From little acorns a Phoenix rises.

Amanda-jayne Parfitt

Presentation by *BookLeaf Publishing*

Web: www.bookleafpub.com

E-mail: info@bookleafpub.com

ISBN: 9789357617222

First edition 2022

To my rock of a husband and two gorgeous children....

You planted the acorns!

That grew the oak tree the Phoenix sits in.

ACKNOWLEDGEMENT

To all the friends family and foes who gave me inspiration! I acknowledge you .

PREFACE

This book is an eclectic mix of poetry....some written from experience....some written from inspiration....some written from hope but all written for you dear reader to enjoy.
Sit ....be comfortable....be present....open the pages and take a piece of me with you.

The Writer

She writes.
Journalists words,
Her pen cutting into the souls
Of those she writes about.
Harsh words of today's news
That tomorrow
Are grease stained and dripping vinegar.
Forgotten by some,
Yet haunting others.
Sometimes she puts the fountain pen down,
It's cutting tip inked and ready.
Picking up a biro
She writes smooth rolling words
Words of love.....seduction.....romance..
On the backs of her cigarette packets,bills and
sweet wrappers.
Her words intertwined with fat content
And final reminders.
Soft words mingling with a health warning
For those in tomorrows news.

Indianna star

We waited,
Anxious,
Anticipating,
Alert for any change
To our mare.

We checked her,
Fed her,nurtured her.
Poked and prodded her.

All this she accepted gracefully,
Always the lady.
We discussed tactics,
The birth,
The symptons,
Distress of the foal.

We were prepared.
Meticulous in our plans.
The date precise.
The build up beginning
Just weeks to go.

We were eager
But not as eager as her!

When we visited
To check
We found her.
A little bundle of brown and white.
She had ruined our plans,
Arrived on her own ,
Unaided,unhurt,uneventful.
In her eagerness for life.

The Promise

Flashing a smile of charms.
Green eyes alight with passion.
Promises of love
Seduction,
Fire,
And a wicked laugh.

No gold band.
But
A ring of white
On unweathered skin.
And that
Told everything.

Gathering Dust

It sits there
Unused.
The half empty pot.
The face cream she will not use again.
Her fingerprint still embedded
A promise of tomorrow.
Her dresses
Gone to charity.
Her shoes
Will fit other feet.
Her pearls will warm to others skin.
Memories for her children,grandchildren.
A little part of her....
To remind us.

Her pots and pans
Will boil for us.
Her recipe books
Will speak to us in her handwriting.
Reminders of her face,
Her love,
Her heart.
But her face cream
Half empty
Dust covered.

Who will use her face cream
Now that nana is gone.

Cest le vie!

I am still trying you know.
Trying to get my foot off the ground.
My head in the clouds.
My foot lifts,
My hand clasps the ladder.
Then slips again
And I end up
Down
With a splinter in my hand
To show I tried.

The Mare

She grieves.
She is not human
But animal
Yet her grief is bare.

She paces her stable,
Nickering soft melodies
To her two dead foals.

She paces and frets,
Sweat covers her,
Her grief is raw.

She is blood stained
And dripping milk.

She is weeping
Red milky tears
For her babies.

She is not human
But animal
And she grieves.

Dirty Dishes

He often watched her at the sink,
His scuffed school shoes
Kicking the table legs.

Her back was too him
Hastily tied apron strings
Unravelling and dangling.

Her back moving as she sobbed.
Quietly
Into the soap suds.
Her hands washing the same dish
Over and over again.

His father
He knew had left
His alcoholic love calling him.

So he sat and watched her.
School shoes banging rhythmically on the table.
As the blood from her broken nose
Dripped
Into the dirty dishwater.

Valley children

They walked hand in hand
Along the river bank.
Loves young dream!
Her red ponytail swishing.
His ropey muscles on display.
Matching tattoos and vodka bottles.
They could never have foreseen
The tragedy to come,
As they fumbled
Awkward in the long grass.
Twas the way around 'ere.
They were valleys children after all!

Now months on
She sits
Growing monthly
And the boy
Long gone.
Buried six feet under.
Courtesy of her brothers.
They had sworn revenge !
But they hadn't foreseen
When they chased him
To the rivers edge.
That he would slip.

And when they left him
Unconscious
They couldn't of known,
You can drown in an inch of water!
They were valleys children after all!

The poets bag

It's green
And my journals fit in it!

I am the carrier bag queen.
My life in various bags.
Supermarket slogans ablaze.
Thin or thick
They adorn my house.
Hanging on door handles,
Hidden in wardrobes,
Stuffed inside drawers.
Artefacts of my life.
Snapshots
Encased inside.
Lost to the chaos of the carrier bags.

So I bought a bag
My first one!

It's green
And my journals fit in it.
It's my poets bag.

The day the clouds fell down.

A horse can hear a human heartbeat from four
feet away.
They can feel vibe,
Intention.
Slow their heart to beat to yours.
Feel your fear.
Pain.

Did you feel my heart break....
When yours stopped.

Thirty five years
A lifetime of loving you
Under blue skies.

But then the clouds fell down.

I sat with your orange face.
Breathed your last breath with you.

Felt you leave.

A piece of me will always remain.
In that last place,
Where your heart stopped,

And you took your last breath.

And your soul left mine.

Wild fire

I watch them,
Two hearts,
One mind.
Fire in them both.

Wild,
Untamed,
Non conforming.

They move as one
The power of the mare
Absorbed by the girl.

Curly locks bouncing,
They gallop.

Breaths steaming the air.
Laughter carrying in the wind..

Both smiling
Both moving to one goal.
Intently listening ,
Hearing only each others voices.
Speaking a language they created.

They speak in unison
Time and time again.
Ebb and flow of a tide.

A rescue mare
A spirited child.
Bonded.

Unbreakable,
Unstoppable.
Unspoken love.

Saved by each other.

The Foaling

The mare stands.
Patiently letting us examine her.
Watching,
We see the foal in his confinement
Kicking.
Small feet...
Or hocks...
Leaving alien prints in her flanks.

Yet she huffs contentment.
Breath silver in the moonlight.

Face awash with the purple haze,
We leave her in the small hours.
Stumbling across cobbles.

We make tea,
Water boiling.
Putting teabags into stained cups
We plan the future.

Minutes later
We walk back,
Steaming mugs in hands,
An attempt at insomnia.

And on return
We are speechless....

Shrouded in his afterbirth,
Embalmed in blood
Little seahorse head stained pink.

He has arrived.

The Pheonix

She rises,
From every fall,
From every disaster.
Broken wings healing.
Heart beating ,
Passion.
Sparks lighting
Until she erupts
Molten lava consuming all.
And she bursts free of her walls
And once more
Flies.

Healed,
Whole,
Flight,
Freedom,
Life.

But a tidal wave has my phoenix!
She was flying
High
Free.
Happy loved whole again.

And a huge swirling mass of white water
Consumed her.
It grabbed her in powerful jaws.
Crushing.

She fought,
She flew into the waves,
Upwards,
Sideways.
But every flight they broke her.

Took her wings and snapped them.
Took her feathers and stopped the very flight of
her.
Took her once beating heart and stilled it with
fear.
Took her fire and smothered the flames in soapy
waves.
Took her spark and soaked it to oblivion.
Took her ashes with icy breath.
Took her!

Acorns

You gave me acorns once.
Five round little spheres.
You came out of school
Clutching them in grubby little cherub hands.
Face alight with your newly found present for
me.

We put them in the ashtray of the jeep,
To keep them safe.
Because they are magic you said.

They were forgotten about
Until today.
When at my lowest point
Routing in the ashtray for coins!
I found them.

And realise that no matter what
I have acorns.
And my sweet innocent child,
They are magic!
Because they remind me of you
And everything will be o.k
Because I have acorns.

Mighty oak

You gave me acorns once.
Chubby little four year old hands
Clutching five little acorns.

Telling me they are magic.
Always giving me hope.
A dream
A future.
I found them once at my lowest point,
And smiled.

Then I blinked.
Paused for a moment to soak in you.
To live in the now,
Beaches
Surfing
Riding
Rock pooling
Adventures
Treasure hunts
Camping
Shmores and so much more.

Watched you grow
Thrive

Learn.
And before me stood a man.
Tall,mighty,solid,proud.
My oak from an acorn.

And I watch now
As you put down roots
Away from mine.
And spread glorious branches
Over those you love.
And you grow.
From tiny acorns mighty oaks are born.

Bridges

Someone once tried
To put out my spark.

They lost everything
In the fire.

I danced.
Flame hair matching flames.
Fire works in a navy sky.
Swirling
Twirling
Free.

And when it cooled.
I danced on the ashes
Of every bridge I burnt .
And never looked back.

And Just like that
It was not the end,
But the beginning.

Obsidian

She danced around the ashes
Of every bridge
She had burned.
Danced
Wild,
Naked,
Free
In the flames.

She started the fire with a spark.
Phoenix rising
Wings fanning the flames.
Lava erupting from the volcano.

Then she poured icy revenge
Onto the flames.
Turned the lava
To obsidian.

Walked bare foot
Onto the cold dead ashes,
And made trophies
From the volcanic glass,
To hang around her neck.
An albatross
Of the trophy of triumph.

Eggshells

I spent so many years
Walking on eggshells.
Ever fearful
Ever watchful.
Never doing or saying the right thing.
Then one day,
A wise owl
Awoke my pheonix.
And I decided
Enough was enough.
I stamped all over those eggshells.
Crushing fragments beneath my feet.
Those broken pieces cut me deeply.
As I walked away.
But this.
This was the most
Exquisite,
Beautiful,
Pain I had ever felt.
And the bleeding
Made me feel
Whole again.

The Hourglass

One grain falls.
And I am born.

I grow
Learn
Cry
And scream.

Then another grain falls.

I walk
Unsteady
Unsure
Others rebel in my joy.
And I am loved.

Then another grain falls.

I run now
Free
Wild
Over green grass
Mud squishes in my toes.

And another grain falls.

Now I love another.
Two hearts.
One soul
One mind.

And another grain falls.

Now there are three
Now four.
Now whole.
And I am worshipped.

And another grain falls.

Now I see light,
Life.
Purpose,
I grow trees and roots.

And another grain falls.

Now branches leave me.
Roots spread further.
Love is there but left.
Now there is two.

And another grain falls.

Now I ache.
Slower
Wiser
Still happy.

And another grain falls.

Now I sit.
Quiet,
At peace.
Thankful and full.
I am still loved.

And the last grain falls.

The party

He proposed.
She agreed.
Radiantly happy
In her perfect life.
At their engagement party.
They laughed,
And danced.
He told her she was beautiful.
And punched her.
Once.
So she would never forget.

Poetry it will never work!

Poems are full of ghosts,
And memories.
A shadow of another self.
Memories of a different time.
A promise of unspoken words.

Promises of forever
Written in swirling handwritting.

Love letters
With hidden meaning.

Words from centuries ago
Bringing unrequited love to life.

But forever fades,
Love passes
And
You will never see
The poetry you stirred in me.

You will never see
That you had all of me.